CCSS Genre Expository Text

W9-AZT-883

Essential Question
How can scientific knowledge change over time?

MARS

BY YVONNE MORRIN

Throughout history, people have been fascinated by Mars. Ancient people observed a point of red light in the sky and wondered what it might be. Unlike the stars, which were white and appeared to move in an arc every night, this red light wandered around the sky.

The ancient Egyptians called the light Her Desher, meaning "the red one." The Romans called it Mars, after their god of war. Perhaps its red color reminded them of the blood of battle.

Early scientists observed the planet's movement. Later **astronomers** discovered more about Mars using telescopes. Questions still remained. People wondered: What is Mars made of? What shape is it? How big is it? Does it have an **atmosphere**? Is it hot or cold? Could there be life on Mars? Some of these questions are still unanswered today.

Stock Trek/Photodisc/Getty Images

We know Mars as the red planet.

Recent space missions have provided answers to some of these questions. These missions to Mars have added to our knowledge about the planet.

However, there are still questions about Mars that can only be answered by further scientific exploration. Maybe someday, humans will get to visit the red planet and see it for themselves.

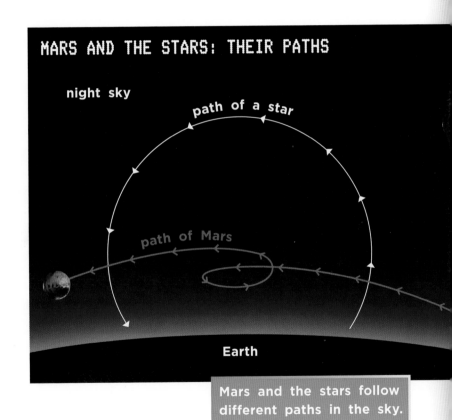

MARS AND THE STARS: THEIR PATHS

night sky

path of a star

path of Mars

Earth

Mars and the stars follow different paths in the sky.

CHAPTER 1

DISCOVERING MARS

Visitors to Mars would find a very hostile place: it is arid, cold, covered in rocks, and seemingly without life. Yet Mars is the planet in our solar system that is most like Earth. It has seasons and an atmosphere, and its day is almost the same length as ours.

COMPARISON BETWEEN MARS AND EARTH

	MARS	EARTH
Average Distance from the Sun	142 million miles	93 million miles
Diameter	4,220 miles	7,926 miles
Length of Day	24 hours, 39 minutes	23 hours, 56 minutes
Length of Year	687 Earth days	365 days
Average Temperature	-81°F	57°F
Atmosphere	Mostly carbon dioxide	Mostly nitrogen and oxygen
Gravity	3/8 that of Earth*	1

* On Mars, you would weigh three-eighths of what you do on Earth.

The facts we know about this fascinating planet have been gathered over time, thanks to the work of astronomers. However, astronomers can make mistakes. Sometimes they have misinterpreted their observations about Mars and drawn the wrong conclusions. Some of their mistaken **theories** include Mars being a hot and fiery place, Mars being covered in thick forests, and even Mars having cities full of people like us!

Because science is flexible, astronomers' ideas can be proven or disproven based on **evidence**. If a theory is disproven, it is replaced with a new theory. As scientific research improves over time, these new theories could also be replaced.

A WORD FROM MARS

The ancient Romans called the planet Mars after their god of war, and although we no longer associate the planet with war, there is still a word in the English language that links the two: *martial.* This word means "relating to war or war-like." For example, martial arts are fighting or defensive sports such as judo and karate.

The diameter of Earth is nearly twice the diameter of Mars.

Before the telescope was invented, approximately 500 years ago, an astronomer named Nicolaus Copernicus used math to figure out that the planets move around the sun. People were shocked because they believed that Earth was the center of the universe. Surely the planets and the sun must orbit Earth! However, Copernicus was right.

In 1609, another astronomer's theories caused a stir. At that time, most people believed that planets orbiting the sun moved in perfect circles. Johannes Kepler used a mathematical calculation to prove that planets move in an oval path, called an **elliptical** orbit.

ELLIPTICAL ORBITS OF PLANETS

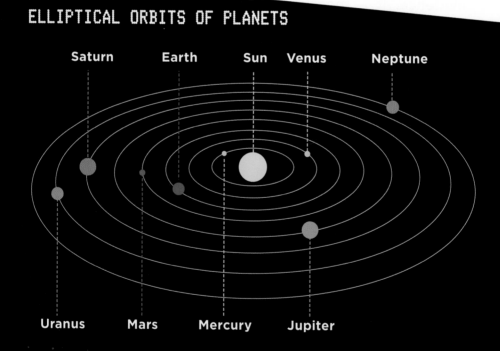

The planets move in elliptical, or oval-shaped, orbits around the sun.

In the same year, another astronomer, Galileo Galilei, became the first person to use an astronomical telescope to observe Mars. His telescope was a very simple device, but it allowed him to see the shape of the planet. As telescope technology developed over time, astronomers observed features on the surface of Mars, such as lines and patches of dark and light.

Early telescopes, such as the one used by Galileo, were basic but still enabled astronomers to learn about Mars.

In 1784, William Herschel, a British astronomer, speculated that some light patches at Mars's poles might be **polar** ice caps, similar to those on Earth. He was right.

Herschel's telescope allowed him to identify more of the red planet's features.

Herschel correctly **deduced** that Mars had an atmosphere. However, his theory that light areas on the surface of Mars were land and dark areas were oceans was wrong. He also thought that having land, oceans, and an atmosphere must mean there is life on Mars.

An Italian astronomer, named Giovanni Schiaparelli, saw lines on Mars. He called them *canali*, which means "channels" in Italian. Channels are natural waterways carved by moving water. However, the word was translated into English as "canals." Canals are waterways that have been dug by people! Because of this mistake, it was reported that Martians had dug canals on Mars. People were very excited. But the lines Schiaparelli thought he had seen never really existed; they were an illusion.

Schiaparelli drew maps of what he thought were channels on Mars.

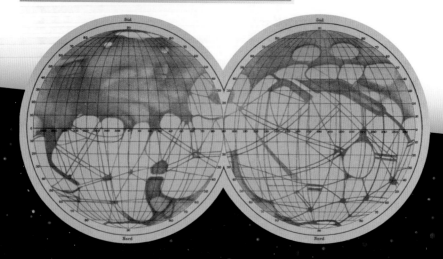

The same year, an astronomer named Asaph Hall made another important and correct discovery. He observed that Mars had two moons. He called them Phobos, meaning "fear" in ancient Greek, and Deimos, meaning "panic." These moons look very different from Earth's moon, which is a sphere. They are much smaller in diameter and have irregular shapes.

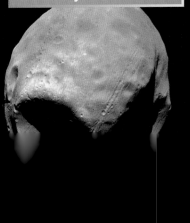

The surface of Phobos has many craters.

EARLY MARS DISCOVERIES

300 B.C.E.
Aristotle sees the moon pass in front of Mars and realizes that Mars is farther away from Earth than the moon is.

1514 C.E.
Copernicus figures out that the planets orbit the sun.

1609 C.E.
Kepler proves that the planets have elliptical orbits.

Galileo observes Mars with a telescope.

1780s C.E.
Herschel figures out that Mars has ice caps and an atmosphere.

1877 C.E.
Schiaparelli thinks he sees lines on Mars's surface.

Hall discovers that Mars has two moons.

CHAPTER 2

ORBITING AND ROVING

For more than 300 years, using a telescope was the only way to observe Mars. That changed with the start of the space program. In 1965, the *Mariner 4* **space probe** flew past Mars, snapping 22 photos of the surface as it passed. These photos showed big craters like the ones on Earth's moon.

In 1971, *Mariner 9* became the first probe to orbit Mars. The first shots showed a massive dust storm, but then came pictures of polar caps, volcanoes, canyons, and old river beds. Mars must have had water! Perhaps it could also have had life.

NASA/Brown RPIF

The photographs taken by space probes allowed scientists to see more detail of Mars's surface.

To find out about life on Mars, the planet's surface needed to be explored. In 1976, two **landers**, called *Viking 1* and *Viking 2*, touched down. The landers had cameras, devices for testing the soil, and equipment to measure the weather. These landers could only send information back to Earth from their landing sites.

The *Pathfinder* mission in 1997 put a **rover** called *Sojourner* on the surface of Mars. This six-wheeled vehicle crawled over the surface, conducting experiments. Since then, many other orbiters, landers, and rovers have been sent to Mars.

EXTREME PLANET

Thanks to the space program, we now know that Mars holds two solar system records: the tallest known mountain and the longest known canyon. Olympus Mons, an extinct volcano, is approximately three times the height of Mount Everest, Earth's tallest mountain. Valles Marineris is a canyon that's nearly 2,500 miles (4,000 kilometers) long. It could stretch across the United States from coast to coast! By comparison, the Grand Canyon is nearly 500 miles (800 kilometers) long.

Dark areas in Valles Marineris are dunes formed by wind.

Olympus Mons is an extinct volcano.

Rover and lander designs are tested in deserts on Earth before going to Mars. There are many criteria used to evaluate the performance of these machines. They must be able to land safely and still function. They must have reliable energy supplies, communication devices, and scientific equipment. Rovers need to be able to move over rough terrain. Their cameras should send accurate picture information.

Because future rovers and landers will use more advanced technology, our knowledge will continue to be updated and we might find an answer to the question: Is there life on Mars?

THE COLORS OF MARS

Camera technology has improved a lot since *Mariner 4* sent photos of Mars back to Earth. Modern photos are much crisper and clearer. One problem with photos is that it is almost impossible to know whether the colors are correct. Colors change depending on the filters that are used and the weather conditions. The Martian sky can look blue, tan, and even pink.

Which is the true color of Mars?

Brand X Pictures/PunchStock/Getty Images

LIFE ON MARS?

Earth is perfectly positioned to support life. It has liquid water to drink, a breathable atmosphere, and just the right amount of sun. Scientists call this the Goldilocks zone. Earth is not too hot, not too cold, but just right!

Although Mars is much colder than Earth, some scientists believe it might be in the Goldilocks zone, too.

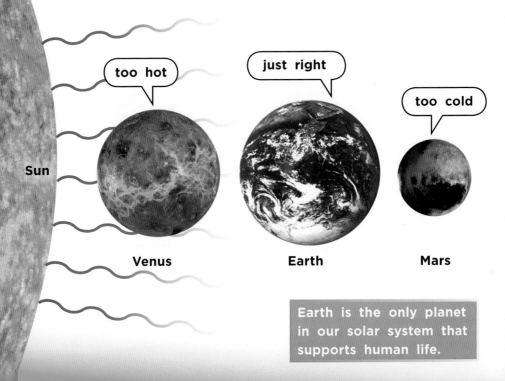

too hot

just right

too cold

Sun

Venus

Earth

Mars

Earth is the only planet in our solar system that supports human life.

We used to think that all life on Earth gets its energy from the sun, but now we know that there are plants and animals that get their energy from chemicals or from the heat of Earth's core. Extremophiles live on Earth in conditions of extreme heat or cold. This has led scientists to think that other extremophiles might live on Mars. Only a small area of Mars has been explored, so this could be possible.

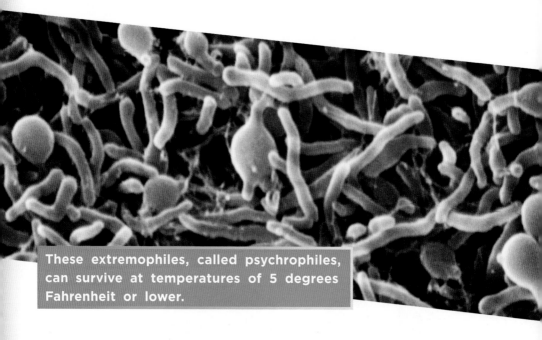

These extremophiles, called psychrophiles, can survive at temperatures of 5 degrees Fahrenheit or lower.

Scientists believe that finding water is the best clue to finding life. Mars has water **vapor** in the atmosphere and frozen water at the poles. Dry riverbeds must have been carved by flowing water in the past. Where did that water go? Could it be under the surface?

Penn State University/Photo Researchers, Inc.

Tiny life forms, such as bacteria, are the most likely forms of life on Mars. In 1984, a **meteorite** thought to be from Mars was found on Earth. Some scientists thought they detected **fossilized** bacteria in the rock, but others disagreed.

FACE ON MARS!

When the *Viking 1* craft sent photos back to Earth in 1976, one of the images appeared to reveal a giant human face on Mars! However, better images of the same feature taken during the 1990s and 2000s show that there is no face.

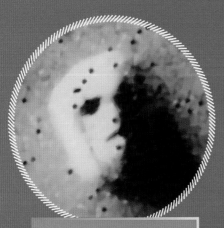

The 1976 *Viking 1* photo appears to show a face on Mars.

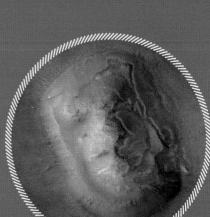

A higher-resolution image from 2001 discredits the theory of a face on Mars.

Mars missions for the future include plans to explore the atmosphere using airplanes and balloons, to dig under the surface using tunnelers, and to return soil and rock samples to Earth. Scientists are interested in learning more about Martian climate and geology, and in looking for any evidence of life on Mars now or in the past.

There are also plans for human exploration of Mars. Humans would need special transportation, protective suits, and places to live. Some people believe humans might live on Mars in the future. Perhaps then, *we* will be the life on Mars!

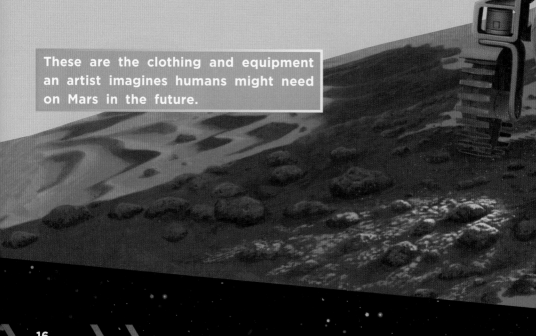

These are the clothing and equipment an artist imagines humans might need on Mars in the future.

NASA Human Spaceflight Collection

Humans have always been interested in observing and understanding their environment. Knowledge of plants, animals, weather, and landscapes helps people to survive.

Despite our growing knowledge of Mars, we are still fascinated by this planet and want to learn more. Perhaps new technology and increased understanding will help humans to explore, adapt to, and even settle on Mars in the future.

Respond to Reading

Summarize

Use important details from *Mars* to summarize how knowledge about Mars has changed over time. Your graphic organizer may help you.

Cause → Effect
→
→
→
→

Text Evidence

1. How can you tell that *Mars* is an expository text? What are some text features that support the information in the text? **GENRE**

2. What caused people to think there was a giant face on Mars? How did new information affect this idea? **CAUSE AND EFFECT**

3. The Greek root *tele* means "far," and the root *scop* means "to look at or observe." Use this information and context clues to define the word *telescopes* on page 2. **GREEK ROOTS**

4. Write about how observation and improving technology caused ideas about Mars to change over time. Be sure to include details from the text in your answer. **WRITE ABOUT READING**

Compare Texts
Read about how understanding science helps a boy enjoy life on Mars.

ZACH
THE MARTIAN

It's never easy being the new kid in school, but Zach was sure that being the new kid on the planet was worse!

"Zach's mom is Earth's new ambassador to Mars," the teacher said. Everyone stared at Zach as if he were an alien.

On Earth, Zach was of average height, but the Mars kids grew tall and willowy due to the planet's low gravity. Zach groaned when the class went to play basketball. He was no match for these giants.

Zach couldn't control his movements. It had taken two weeks on Mars to master walking in low gravity. Finally, Zach managed to get the ball. He threw it and it hit a teammate, knocking her over.

Illustration: Sole Otero

19

"Zach has worked against Earth's gravity all his life," said the teacher, "so his muscles are more developed than ours. He'll learn to be gentler eventually."

Zach was mortified. "I need to get some fresh air," he told himself, but there was none. The whole colony was covered in a giant dome, filled with recycled air.

"Are you okay?" a voice asked. It was Gemma, the girl who was hit by the ball.

"I should be asking you that," he said.

She smiled. "I'm fine. It must be hard coming to Mars. I was born here, so I didn't have to adapt. Mars isn't really so bad. This afternoon, our class is working in the gardens."

Zach was surprised when his class went into a large greenhouse, full of fresh fruits and vegetables, all grown hydroponically.

"See," Gemma said as the class checked the water solutions, "we're making new discoveries all the time. We're getting better at growing food and recycling water and air."

When class finished, Gemma and Zach went outside under the dome. Zach was amazed to see a trampoline. Gemma got on and flipped graceful somersaults. Then Zach climbed on. He bounced tentatively at first, but soon the combination of his greater muscle power and the low gravity sent him higher and higher. He felt like a superhero.

"Maybe it's not so bad," he thought, "being a Martian!"

Illustration: Sole Otero

Make Connections

What kinds of things have the people living on Mars in *Zach the Martian* learned to do better over time? **ESSENTIAL QUESTION**

How would living on Mars like the characters do in *Zach the Martian* allow us to answer some of the questions people asked in *Mars*? **TEXT TO TEXT**

Glossary

astronomers *(uh-STRON-uh-muhrz)* people who observe and study outer space *(page 2)*

atmosphere *(AT-muhs-feer)* the layer of gas surrounding a planet *(page 2)*

deduced *(di-DEWST)* figured out something by using facts you already know *(page 8)*

elliptical *(i-LIP-ti-kuhl)* shaped like an oval *(page 6)*

evidence *(EV-i-dens)* something that helps us prove that something else is true *(page 5)*

fossilized *(FOS-uh-lighzd)* changed into a fossil, or a preserved trace of a living thing from long ago *(page 15)*

landers *(LAND-uhrz)* space vehicles designed to land on a planet *(page 11)*

meteorite *(MEE-tee-uh-right)* a piece of rock or metal that has fallen to Earth from outer space *(page 15)*

polar *(POH-luhr)* relating to a pole or the region around a pole *(page 7)*

rover *(ROH-vuhr)* wheeled machine that collects data on the surface of a planet *(page 11)*

space probe *(SPAYS prohb)* an unmanned spacecraft designed to explore space and send data back to Earth *(page 10)*

theories *(THEE-uh-reez)* ideas that have not been proven *(page 5)*

vapor *(VAY-puhr)* gaseous particles suspended in the air *(page 14)*

Index

Focus on Science

Purpose To give students a chance to see Mars for themselves

Procedure

Step 1 With a partner or on your own, use the Internet to research when you can observe Mars from where you live.

Step 2 Talk to an adult at home and pick a night when you can all go out to view Mars together.

Step 3 Take a notebook with you and draw what you see. Where is Mars in the sky? Try to use landmarks on the ground to help you draw Mars in the right place. See if you can go outside a few hours later to look for Mars again. Do you think it will be in the same spot? Why or why not?

Step 4 Share your observations with the rest of the class.

Conclusion What did you notice about Mars? How was it like, or not like, what you expected? If there's a planetarium or observatory near where you live, consider visiting so you can look at Mars through a telescope. How do you think the view through the telescope would compare with your view at home?